Subliminal Attraction

Subliminal Attraction

Franck Olivier Houngnikpo

Village Tales Publishing

USA

Published in the United States by:
Village Tales Publishing
Lawrenceville, GA

A catalog record for this book is available from the Library of Congress:
LCCN: 2018947547
ISBN-13: 9781945408236

Book Layout and Cover by OASS

Printed in the United States

This book is dedicated to:

Lucrece Houngnikpo, Nee Ayihou

And

Thomas Franklin Houngnikpo

ACKNOWLEDGEMENT

This work will not have seen the daylight of print without the favour of God and various assistance and encouragement from friends and loved ones.

I thank particularly, Mr. Augustine Sherman and Mr. Francois Kwawudade, a professor at Cape Coast University in Ghana, for his amazing work in proofreading this book.

I shall forever remain grateful to Madame Chantal Saizonou for her unconditional support and Isidore B. Vieira, my uncle.

I thank Patrick Agoli-Agbo, Herbert Rodrigue Amoussou-Chouh, Canique Rodinard Cakpo, Zacharie Mbaiadoum Ngarabe, Andrew Cephas Abankwe and Ambroise Tossou.

FOREWORD

It is true that deception, heartbreaking, lies, ambitions, loss of confidence and particularly the world we are living in nowadays, so crazy and weird made it hard to believe in true love. This simply results in doing more harm to one another, almost close to the life of animals in a jungle where everyone is so cautious and on the alert.

That notwithstanding, believing that true love no longer exists at all, and that all men and women are alike, is either a mistake or a choice; the former is corrigible while the latter ought to be fought.

'*Subliminal Attraction*' is a nonfiction book which goes against every claim that love is unreal by viewing a genuine experience of how a man encountered true love and ceased his chance. They could remain happy forever.

Chapter 1

All started when there was no more hope, no more laughter. It started while I had no idea of how life would treat me or go on, what my life would be like in the near future. Everything commenced with a broken heart while I didn't even have a clue as to how it would be mended again.

Before I got to that point, there are some few things I ought to disclose to you first. But if you have never been in love, if you never had that soft heart to house someone's daughter inside, you might not get me right. All I mean is that it takes someone who has been in a serious relationship to understand me. I am neither talking about a boyfriend and girlfriend thing, nor hooking out which only aim at chilling and sleeping together. I am talking about a real feeling, a relationship that is destined to a bright tomorrow.

Anyway, I won't blame you if you've never had such a relationship or experience, that amazing feeling because I know perfectly well how hard it is nowadays to get the perfect match. Besides, no one is ready for it since we all have in mind that all women are the same. Likewise, the ladies also think the same: all men are the same.

No matter how hard it is scarce nowadays to meet a serious lady or man, I do believe there are some out there with a golden heart. Even though we keep on being deceived, cheated on and misled, I still insist in believing they are some men and women with a particular conviction and credence. I trust the Lord, in the fact that there is always an exception in every case. That exception is what I want, ache for and wish every minute.

For more than two years, coming from different horizons in search of a better life, we met. Things happened so fast and brought us together in the name of love. We spent lovely times together and I thought she would be my last. She accepted my proposal straight away, which made my heart, and my spirit, joyous.

Alas, no. There was no future for what I planned; no hope to lift up my dreams. All my hope sank and my dreams faded away. The lady I spent several years with, would never marry me in spite of all the love, and affection, we seemed to share.

Do not go there, for I know what is going on in your twisted mind. She didn't cheat on me, but she wasn't just meant for me. She was destined to someone else, a future I shouldn't be part of.

She came from somewhere in Central Africa, where she returned to after her studies. She also went back because she had to tell her parents about me, prepare the way before I showed up. That was the reason why she left; that was the mission she expected to accomplish, before things fell apart.

Her first days afar were stimulating, and hopeful, because we were still in touch; we chatted on the phone almost every day and that was it. Then I felt her absence when it came to cooking, cleaning, washing and so forth, because I had already lost the habit of doing them. For quite a time, I managed to overcome it for the sake of regaining my own stability.

Thus, I was getting ready for everything needed to make her my wife, though it wasn't easy for me. My modest person could not afford certain stuffs at the due moment; but I was on it.

Then came the ominous day on which I discovered I wasn't, in fact, welcome in that household. They proved it to me in many ways possible, even though their daughter was still madly in love with me. As a man, I refused to forsake her. I wanted to fight for what I believed in, and also for the love I shared with their daughter. I objected to letting it go because my mind was only on her, and no one else. The situation got tougher and tougher, and I was at a complete lost. I then asked her to come back to me so that we handle things over here our own way, before any breakthrough. I almost begged her to join me but she disagreed with me. I tried again but she refused to obey. I might not be right in my decision back then but for me, it was the only way to escape from her parents' twisted mindset. She might have her reasons too, but I was just trying to save what we built together. The more I thought, the tougher it got and at that point, I could feel my heart quaking inside my chest as if it would soon ooze with pain.

When these moments come in a man's life, he needs help; someone with elephant's ears to listen and to talk to. I then turned to the most wonderful people I had, people to whom I explained things to, and the mess in which I was. They all listened to me with a keen interest, advised me according to their comprehension and experience. They didn't force me into doing anything; even my father and mother did not force me. They just counseled me and left me to my fate. After then, I made a decision because I needed to. I couldn't continue living in the dwaal. It was either I force that relationship which the parents didn't agree on, and bear the consequences—good or bad—or I abandon everything, knowing that I would have to start it all over again. In one way or the other, I ought to make up my mind before I ended up wretched.

Many weeks passed with countless sleepless nights, long days of reflection and illusion when I finally decided what to do with my future, my life. I chose to terminate our relationship even though it hurt. I thought I'd better get hurt earlier than later. I managed to convince her with tangible reasons, yet she wasn't totally in the net. She would rather prefer that we force, that we go against her parents' will if need be. Under no circumstance would I force a lady to be with me against her parents' or her own wish.

How does it feel?

I felt sad, devastated, and empty. I was hurt as if I caught her with another man in our matrimonial bed, but that wasn't the case. I might not have cried, but my heart wept in silence. I was lost, and never thought anything could ever make me happy. My profession, and pastime, became my only hope. As a lecturer, I was obliged to force a smile and laugh every day in the presence of my students knowing very well that it was all fake. The bottom line is, that they shouldn't be victims of my acrimony. Hence, I made sure I kept my composure any time I entered the lecture hall to educate those innocent students.

She felt sad, devastated and empty. She was also hurt and betrayed by my decision that she judged unfair and too harsh. She called me back several times later to make up, to come and join me if necessary. Nonetheless, I rejected it because it was too late. That was the time she had decided to do anything at all, and I wondered why not before. Should she let things get worse before standing?

Month after month, day after day, I prayed to God to forgive me if I ever did wrong, if my decision was premeditated or rude. I also prayed that the Almighty help Linda through the hard time we all put her through, her parents first, followed by me. Being very far from each other, only God knew what she suffered.

Looking at situations, I did believe we could get another chance, coming across partners that would fit us adequately. We all deserved it. In spite of my little faith, I asked God to favor us.

Two good years passed, and I remained a bachelor. My fear by then was whether I would remain a bachelor, or whether I would be able to meet another lady just like Linda, or even better.

Chapter 2

My age was climbing the ladder like a bird soaring higher and I was still alone. My only companions were my work and studies. None of the women I saw day after day pleased me, on the contrary they scared the hell out of me.

If I wanted a lady to hang out with, it was easy. If I wanted to spend time with someone, that wouldn't be a problem. If I had needed sex, it would have been a piece of cake.

I met ladies of all types every single day. The dressing is catastrophic with their bodies, especially their intimate parts being exposed to the whole world. Their excessive make-up that looks like a colorful painting one is desperate to sell. The way they talked, the friends they made were all rebuking; too much for me to stand.

Women no longer have respect for themselves, their parents not to talk about their surroundings, how would they respect you the husband?

Women care less about love as far as there is money. They cherish gender equality meanwhile they refuse to work hard as much as men do.

Women no longer believe in God or in life after death, or repentance. It is unfortunate as they live their life full of sins in which they purposely indulged.

I saw women who had no job driving fancy cars, eating in chic restaurants, living in outstanding houses because they always lured some men, mostly wealthy men, who could not stay faithful to their wives, or control their libido into their snare. I saw ladies sleeping with their superiors and bosses just to take advantage of them, and after all impose themselves. They would use outside products until they bleached; they all wanted to become fair: white, yellow.... So, you see some of them with many different colors at the same time on various parts of their bodies; colors of course because that is not their complexion. I remember those ladies with the fingernails made up, colorfully designed as if they never touched anything at home. They had to have housemaids to get everything done for them, including washing their pants. The bogus eyelashes, fake butt, and boobs became a fashion; whatever.

The worst is yet to come, and I ask myself where the world is heading to. Children that parents no longer have control on, yet they are still very young. If I should marry a lady who walks naked, I'd rather stay alone. No responsible woman can carry herself that way. I saw a lot of things with women that got me really scared; it was awful.

Within that time, many ladies were interested in me in various ways. Some wanted me for my little money and others because I was working. Some others wanted me for the simple fact of counting me among their numerous suitors, while many would love to be with me because of my social status. I might not be rich, but I have a name that people respect once they hear it.

Those of my students who wished to be with me were mostly after free marks, or for me to help them with their home assignments. One way or the other, they were all after ephemeral interest. My point is that none of them proved to me that she wanted to be with me for a serious relationship, none of them showed me real love and care. I couldn't feel any promise and expectation in a future with them.

Too bad!

One after the other, I avoided them all for what I ached for was greater than what they pursued. Those ladies were just thinking of the present and not the future, especially the beautiful ones. They think their beauty, either fake or God given, will be eternal. I didn't want any of that. And I concentrated on most important issues at hand, praying for the rest to happen.

I must confess that I was really tempted to call Linda and tell her how much I loved her and wanted her back. I almost sent her a message to say how sorry I was. While thinking about it, I got lost in those great moments we had had together, and with a smile on my face, I did not know when I shed tears. Probably because the emotion was stronger than me, and I slipped.

Nevertheless, I exercised calm and patience. I stood strong and firm. I preferred not to stir up the fire logs; which I was battling to extinguish. Calling, or writing to her at that moment might be fatal for me.

I didn't do it.

Chapter 3

Since my last misadventure, I promised myself that I will never date an outsider again; except a woman from my land. I'd better date a woman with whom I speak the same language, and respect almost the same tradition; not a woman who knows nothing about me, and doesn't mind left from right, as far as my hometown customs and traditions are concerned. Linda and I faced those kinds of divisions and misunderstanding.

One day, while the thick clouds made the sky dull and gloomy, the half-moon also tried to impose itself with its dim beams. I did close for the maddened day I had, and lying in bed after dinner, very exhausted. I didn't want to involve myself in doing anything at all;

neither writing, nor reading as I often did. I was lost in my thought, thinking about so many things one at a time. My telephone suddenly vibrated and drew my attention. I should rather say, it brought me back to my senses. It was a WhatsApp message. I slid down the screen and logged in. There was that recent message sent to me by an unknown number.

Unknown number: Toc! Toc! Toc! I'm back oh.

Though I didn't know the number texting to me, I understood that it was someone I knew very well, considering the content of the message he or she sent me. It bothered my mind to recall the owner of the number, but I couldn't. Admitting I really forgot who it was, I was curious to find out.

Me: *Hello.*
Unknown number: *Hi.*
Me: *Who is it, please?*
Unknown number: *It is HOPE, have you forgotten me?*
Me: *Ah, yes. Sorry dear. Welcome back.*
Unknown number: *Thanks.*
Me: *Good. Send me one of your pictures, please. Let me see your face, I missed it.*
Unknown number: *Ok.*

Ok, the name sure sounded familiar to me, but I couldn't picture the person in my mind. For that reason, I asked for her picture to be certain, so that I could clearly identify my guest. After two minutes, she sent me an angelic picture which beautified my mind. She was gorgeous. Automatically, I went into my setting to save her number with her name.

> **Me:** *Nice picture... Welcome back.*
> **Hope:** *Thanks.*

Neither Hope nor I wrote a word after that brief discussion. I could barely explain how I slept off that night. I have just remembered that we had another discussion the following morning. I buzzed her first that dawn, hardly had it been 7 a.m.

> **Me:** *Good morning princess. Did you sleep well? There is a group of debate, quotation and proverbs that I would like you to join, if you don't mind.*
> **Hope:** *Good morning. I am in.*
> **Me:** *Ok. How are you this morning?*
> **Hope:** *Fine. Today sounds better.*
> **Me:** *And, tomorrow will be much better.*

On the third day, our conversation was quite longer than the previous because we were more relax, and discussed some few things. Everything started when I discovered the sadly touching profile she put on her wall. It stated that she missed him a lot. I guessed she was talking about her boyfriend or husband, whatever. It was half past six.

> **Me:** *Oh, sorry. Try to call him.*
> **Hope:** *Tcho! (Interjection for pity in Fon, our local language) If only I could.*
> **Me:** *Why not, Hope?*

Hope: *His lines are all off since Wednesday. Apart from that, it is not the only reason why I am sad and alone.*
Me: *Why, then?*
Hope: *My family, I miss my sister, especially now that she has given birth and I am not around to help her.*
Me: *Hope, give me one hour. I will be back for you.*
Hope: *Ok.*

Then I logged off for a certain reason I can't remember now. But after one and half hours, I reappeared and messaged her.

Me: *I am back.*
Hope: *More than one hour.*
Me: *Kinkinlin! (Interjection for sorry, or please, in Fon), sorry.*
Hope: *No problem.*
Me: *So, has your sister given birth?*
Hope: *Yes, please.*
Me: *Where is she now?*
Hope: *In Benin Republic.*
Me: *It isn't that far, why don't you go to pay her a visit?*
Hope: *Yes, I could. But it is ok now.*
Me: *You are right. Find the way to get closer to her.*
Hope: *There come times like that when we wish to be by our beloved ones.*
Me: *That is, exactly.*

I went into my pictures file and selected some funny, relaxing and consoling pictures that I sent her just to make her smile a while. I wanted to alter her mood as she was feeling lonely and sad. I wasn't sure how to succeed, but that was what oozed into my mind. I surely succeeded in making her shine, I thought. Some minutes later, I swiftly changed the topic on purpose.

> **Me:** *Have you eaten tonight?*
> **Hope:** *Yes, I have.*
> **Me:** *Good. I pray that by tomorrow your husband calls you.*
> **Hope:** *I hope so.*
> **Me:** *Keep calm, he would.*
> **Hope:** *Thank you.*
> *(She sent some smileys showing her joy.)*

It was almost 9 p.m., and I hadn't prepared my lecture for the following morning yet. I then logged out without saying bye to Hope in order to focus on my lecture.

At this point, you are all curious to know more about Hope. Well, I will tell you.

Chapter 4

I was once a member of a great association of students and trainees. Then, I became the president in 2014. I learnt what leadership was all about, and drew my own lessons after the ups and downs; the positive and negative circumstances I went through. Even though the gain here wasn't about money, I surely got it profitably. I met great authorities and leaders, and finally became friends with some of them till now.

Owing to my leadership, responsibility, and role I played at the summit of that association, my name flew farther. Of course, an honor I shared with every single member of my bureau by then, and all those upright men who supported me. Even when I ceased being their leader, I then turned out to be a role model to some, to counsel and hearten them on certain association matters, as well as personal at times.

One Saturday, I attended the monthly meeting we always had, for the item on the agenda was so important, and every good member of the community was meant to be present. Students came from everywhere to be part of it; countless, where those who came for the first time because they'd heard of it.

Nothing changed much compared to when I was leading. The leaders took the speech and explained the motives of our presence, questions were being asked, and interventions were booming from every corner in that hall. I was seated coyly at the back of the rowdy crowd, watching every little move they were making, men and women, newcomers and commoners. I could say it was the most vibrant and interesting meeting I ever attended since I was out of office.

A lady particularly set the hall on fire that very evening. She was sitting at a distance from me in a way that I could barely see her from the back, and quite on profile. I was able to see her clearly when she approached me after the meeting. She wore a brown t-shirt, striped white on a gray skirt, that modestly descended to her knees. She was such a beauty that God designed with a willing heart. Her round face with a pointed nose, her eyes sparkling like stars, were slightly protected with some bold eyelashes. Her shapely beauteous chest had already gotten me confused, but I tried as much as I could to be a man; not to talk of her smile whenever the secretary of the association asked her to face the public and addressed them. Her fine backside responded to every move she made. Her look and dress, everything was just as natural as the nature. Moreover, her eloquence and persuasiveness gave me goose pimples as I love her fluency; no doubt she was indeed educated.

Who is the man behind that gracious woman? I wondered.

Whoever it might be, that humble woman belongs to the luckiest guy in the world, I thought by the way. And then, I awkwardly thought how happy I would be having such precious living being beside me. In fact, that was my manly instinct, nothing more because she definitely belonged to someone already. She had a ring on her ring finger, symbol of her engagement, I thought.

The meeting ended around 6 p.m., and there she came to me like an angel from heaven. What could she be looking for? I had no idea. We greeted and she introduced herself to me in my local language (fon); that is how I knew that we even came from the same city. Besides, her name sounded perfect to me: "Hope". Before I introduced myself as she did, the lady stopped me with a grin on the face.

"There is no need, Mr. President, I know you."

Should I say I was surprised? Not really, because people know me, and some have heard my name, while I don't know them. Hope came to me for a job, just anything at all, for her in order not to stay idle indoors all day long. People might have told her that I could help. I gave her my word, gave her my telephone number for us to be in touch till I got her something; which I did.

We had some discussions on WhatsApp later on regarding the job issue and other stuff, just the kind of care and attention I promised to give her, to help her do her job well.

I also knew Hope was a great woman with a bright future. I encouraged her a lot, and advised her as much as I could. That was how we became real friends.

When I lost my phone I also lost her contact information, with that of many others. At that same time, her mobile phone got broken and we couldn't chat any more. I thought I would meet her at our next meeting, unfortunately she couldn't make it. I asked some people who were supposed to know her whereabouts, but they also knew nothing. I then realized I was too worried about her, which wasn't normal. For almost three months, we couldn't get in touch, and naturally I forgot her. After those three months, I felt normal then, because she was no longer in my head. Life went on.

After a long day of hard work, with highs and lows, and built-up tension, I got home very tired. I managed to bath and got some food to eat. There I was in bed that night when she wrote to me: Toc! Toc! Toc! That was how we renewed the contact; meaning, I had her number anew.

Chapter 5

Everyone plans and writes down things he or she wants, and expects within the year. We fight hard to get them achieved by God's grace, and our own endeavor. Considering how difficult the previous year was, I could not achieve all my targets. November thirty-first night was my judgment day. I judged myself asking so many questions. I needed to answer to myself about how I got to achieve some things, and why I wasn't able to build others. Sleep was far away as I felt like there was a burden on my chest.

I thanked the Almighty for keeping me strong and healthy, which was actually the most important of all requests. I did pretty well in my studies, got promotion at work, and received new and broader knowledge. I made new friends and families. Those achievements could've been enough but as human, we are unsatisfied. I knew many were unable to reach where I had reached; I thought I should be appreciative then.

Besides, I encountered several hardships along the way. I failed to accomplish some projects that are very important to me because of lack of direction and means. I wished I had been engaged by then, and even had a child before the end of the year, but I wasn't able to succeed in doing that. And the only project I was still struggling to accomplish was my trip to Europe.

It was 1 a.m., December first, when I was making my last plans and wishes; in that deep night, alone in my room and sleepless. I rather felt like drinking coffee, which I served myself with, and grabbed my mobile phone. When I logged onto WhatsApp, all my friends were deep asleep, because no one was online. I checked again, and noticed Hope was online. I decided to leave her a message in case she was not sleeping.

> **Me:** *Hi, Hope.*
> **Hope:** *Hi President, how are you?*
> **Me:** *I am great. What are you thinking of? Aren't you sleeping?*
> **Hope:** *Nothing. It is all because of this city, the heat is too much. No sleep.*
> **Me:** *Don't you have light?*
> **Hope:** *I do.*
> **Me:** *Don't you have a fan or an air-conditioner?*
> **Hope:** *My fan could only blow the heat inside the room. It is not helping.*
> **Me:** *Sorry, dear. This is Accra for us.*

We indulged into commenting on some pictures I had sent her, and those she also sent me. We spent a great deal of time online that late night, full of joy and emotion.

On the second and third of December, Hope and I chatted briefly, and that was it; nothing much to talk about anyway.

On the tenth of December, I started:

> *Me: Hi dear, how are you?*
> *Hope: I'm fine, and you?*
> *Me: Cool! Long time.*

In fact, it wasn't that long but frankly, that was how I felt. So I thought I should express it. Luckily, she did not have any problem with my expression.

> *Hope: Yes. I didn't see you at Tata Christa's graduation.*

Tata Christa was a member of the students' association board. She graduated and I could not be there, not because I didn't want to, but simply because I was out of town.

> *Me: Yeah, I was quite busy. Sorry.*
> *Hope: I hope everything is fine now.*
> *Me: Thank God, and thank you.*
> *Hope: Cool.*
> *Me: Are you free this evening?*
> *Hope: Yep.*
> *Me: Can we meet at Abeka Junction, exactly at 3:23 p.m.?*

Yeah, it might seem funny, but I was damn serious about the time I gave. Each minute with me counts, and I do not play with it. Hope had never heard of timing like that before. She laughed and laughed, thinking I might be joking. She accepted to be there in time when I emphasized: *Come on time. Time is what I don't have. Please.*

There, she impressed me, I must confess, showing up at the exact time I gave her. I took her to the place I got for her to start work.

She was very excited about it, and this was the message she sent me when she got home that evening:

> *Hope: Good evening, President. I have just reached home. From the bottom of my heart, thank you for everything.*
> *Me: Never mind. I wish you took care of it knowing that it might open other doors for you.*
> *Hope: Count on me, President.*
> *Me: Certainly.*
> *Hope: As long as I have people like you around, I am not scared.*
> *Me: I am nobody dear, just helping.*
> *Hope: I would disturb you from time to time. I guess with regular pieces of advice, I will be able to make it.*
> *Me: I know you can. And if you ever need my help, do not hesitate....*
> *Hope: Ok.*

We both logged out before 8 p.m. that night, and met again the following day at six minutes past six.

She sent me a text message first.

Hope: Good evening, President. How are you? I have snatched your profile picture without your permission... in one word, I have stolen it, please do not be angry. Thanks.

When I saw her message, I wondered why she was telling me about it. I smiled. I then replied her not to worry.

Me: How is your day?
Hope: Good. Are you ready for tomorrow's journey?
Me: More or less. I am having some terrible headache and a cold.
Hope: Pity, oh; all of it for you alone?
Me: Yes, dear, but it is ok.
Hope: How about medicines?
Me: Herbal, yes. For the white man, no.
Hope: So are we in the same boat. I prefer tisane too.
Me: Ok then, it is far better.

Chapter 6

December fourteen, earlier in the morning, I travelled to Benin Republic where I was meant to settle certain issues and important cases I was working on. Rushing here and there to get a visa was part of it, and mainly part of my end of year projects.

Oddly, that project I involved myself into was a huge one, little did I know. I must confess that I spent more money on that travelling plan that I had ever expected without counting the to and fro. Ambrose is a good friend of mine that I really thank, by the way, for all his assistance, especially when the only closest country where I could travel to for a visa was Nigeria.

Oh, hell, no! Not Nigeria.

I hated that country. In fact, I promised myself that never would I go there in my life. My father would have been struck to death on that road, when their bus had been attacked with shots. He could barely explain how he came home alive, while other passengers were injured. But you see, that was just how I felt and what I wanted. I then forgot that God could plan things His own way. If He does it for reasons our human nature cannot comprehend, plan things otherwise, they will happen to us, and truly I felt betrayed by my God.

I had never been to Nigeria before that announcement, but I heard so many weird things about that country, things which in general aren't good. I heard how dangerous the country is: their people, culture, belief and behavior. Considering the large number of population in Nigeria, some vices such as theft, violence, betrayal, and African witchcraft are frequent there. God knows I was terribly afraid.

I gathered all my papers and was readily set for the trip with my friend Ambrose. We took off the following day earlier in the morning. Once we got to Seme, the first Nigerian boarder town, I noticed an incredible change of atmosphere: the movement, the language, the dressing, hawkers; even the look on the face of their custom officers, and I knew I was about to enter another world. I've crossed many borders in my life, but crossing Nigeria's border was the strangest of all. Though I had all my papers ready, I still spent a lot of money due to certain alibis they always presented with the only aim of extorting something from us. As long as you do not cooperate, they would waste your time for no concrete reason at all. Honestly, I did not see the dangerous face that had always been pictured, so far thanks to my friend's pals at the border. That guy was fast, bold and determined. He managed to let us cross the border without much difficulty as long as he also had his share because we were meant to pay him some amount.

After that, we boarded a car for the city called, Lagos. Crossing the border was as if I was relieved from a great burden.

I sighed heavily telling Ambrose, "Finally, we are through."

He looked at me and smirked at my innocent thought. "It was just the beginning my friend," he replied. "Wait and see how bothersome the road to Lagos is."

"Again," I asked, surprisingly.

"Yes, again. But don't worry, nothing will happen to us. Believe me."

I was indeed worried to the extent he couldn't even imagine. To be honest, I would have disappeared from the country back to wherever I set off from, if I'd had such power. Nevertheless, I thought I was on the road of no return, I ought to be stout.

As a man, I kept my cool and focused, praying every minute for our safety. We departed as soon as the car got full and we were the only Francophones inside. I got more worried that they might intend to use us for money ritual, but on the contrary they assisted us a lot on our way going.

We were stopped every one kilometer for no apparent reason. Their uniforms were so different that I couldn't really identify who was doing what. While some of them were checking the boot, others were controlling the driver's papers. Some also were questioning us about unnecessary things, and even made us alight, trying to intimidate us. That was how we had been stopping every five minutes of drive to Lagos. It was my first time of hearing a policeman saying, "Having all your papers means nothing to me. Do something, because I do not eat papers."

As we were driving close to a certain check point, although we had all our correct papers, the driver stopped by the roadside asking my friend and me to alight. He advised as to use a taxi-motor commonly called, Okada, in Nigeria to cross that particular part of the road, otherwise, we would be too much disturbed; which would not only cost us much expense, but also waste time. We might have enough money to lavish, but he certainly didn't want to waste time.

According to my friend, we'd better follow his plan. And as long as Ambrose had no problem crossing that way, what could I say. We did as the driver said, and were out of trouble.

I supposed my friend knew it all the way, and every time I got astonished, he would just smile at me and whisper to my ear, "Do not worry my brother. Let's go!"

Under those circumstances, I went to Nigeria. Once inside the country, I felt more relaxed. I could see why it is considered the most populous country in Africa.

We obtained the most necessary documents, by God's grace, and we returned the same day, very late at night though. Twice, again I went back to that country going through the same fuss, which I almost got used to. I did submit my papers finally, expecting the European visa inside.

I obviously had a rough time, but I remember there were always messages of hope, encouragement, wisdom, and attention waiting for me on WhatsApp. They were all from my friend, Hope, but a few from my parents and friends. She kept in touch with me as if she was my wife while she wasn't. And, little by little, I started paying more attention to her as well. But deep inside my heart, I never nourish the idea of dating her. She was engaged and had a ring.

On December twenty-fourth, which happened to be Christmas Eve, Hope and I had engaged into a particular topic for the very first time.

Me: *Do you think there is love nowadays?*
Hope: *Incontestably, yes, my President.*
Me: *But it is scarce, right?*
Hope: *No, not scarce.*
Me: *Are you serious?*
Hope: *Of course I am. Our filthy behaviors, meanness, and false judgment towards one another make us believe love is uncommon.*
Me: *Have you found it? I mean true love?*
Hope: *Yes, President.*
Me: *So, you are serious about it.*
Hope: *Yes, listen. When you get face to face, the one who loves you, and that you love too, you don't need much effort to make it a success. Be careful, do not pretend to love.*
Me: *Meanwhile, we all pretend nowadays. Few are those who love for real.*
Hope: *All depends on the set goals of everyone. Some men, or women, play with others' feelings for the sake of whatsoever, I don't know. Nevertheless, some engage for real.*
Me: *I couldn't deny that... but contrary to your opinion, I think very few belong to the world of seriousness in relationship.*
Hope: *You might be wrong, President.*

Me: *I believe you.*

Hope: *Have you met some? Do you believe in real love?*

Me: *Yes, I had, but not anymore. She went back to her parents, and now they are plotting to give her into marriage.*

Hope: *To someone else? Another man, you mean?*

Me: *Yes, Hope.*

Hope: *Oops! Parents, too? I suppose, what you both feel prevails. If you think you are ready, why don't you go to meet a reasonable person in her family to talk to? Befriend him, or her, and start the dowry process. Most of all, do not forget to pray. May God give you heart and clear the way.*

Me: *I do understand that. But it is more complicated than that. She is not even from my country.*

Hope: *Oh, more complicated. Really? Then you need to understand their customs, religion, and habits in order to know how to approach them. And, why can't she help? I guess the parents don't want an outsider for her.*

Me: *Correct.*

Hope: *Divergence.*

Me: *Yeah... and, a rich guy too.*

Hope: *Too bad! I was thinking that was in the past.*

Me: *Till now, dear.*

Hope: *It is complicated.*

Me: *I am really hopeless in this issue. Though I know she loves me for real, and trying to oppose to her parents decision, how long will that take? And frankly, due to my travel plans and some other expenses, there is no way to fly to her country now. Moreover, who knows whether my appearance there would change anything as long as I am not well-off.*

That was the very first time my friend and I conducted such an open discussion about my private life. I willingly just told her everything by pouring out my heart, otherwise I might blow up. She gave me ideas, directives, and advice as if she were my mother. Then, she made a point.

> *Hope: What if you look around you? There may be a lady somewhere out there who really loves you and expecting you to notice her. On the other hand, you can ask her to join you, which is not probable, or get her pregnant, another huge risk. I believe we ought to take some drastic decisions at times.*
> *Me: Yes, I guess I have lost her. You were saying there might be someone around me who loves me and so forth, well there is no one.*
> *Hope: Perhaps where you are travelling to... but never shut your heart to love. It shall be well.*
> *Me: Thank you my dear. I shall try all my best.*
> *Hope: And, try to always keep in touch with her.*
> *Me: Anyway, I've never wronged her and, neither has she.*
> *Hope: God is in charge. No room for neither stress, nor sadness, because you are a winner. Follow your dreams and projects for that is the most important and what really defines you. The rest will surely come.*
> *Me: You are right, but I might never get anyone like her.*

That was where I got stranded with full reminiscence of her; I mean my past, our life together. I could clearly recall with details all we promised each other, and where it all landed us. I had sudden goose pimples, but that was all. After some time of silent, she sent me another message.

> *Hope: The only advice I could give you is to follow the best and truthful combats...your dreams.*
> *Me: You are right, gorgeous. That was exactly what everyone told me.*
> *Hope: You could even meet someone who loves you more than her, if you believe. But thinking that she is*

the only one, may decline your eyes and shut your heart. What we want is one thing, and what God wants for us is another.
Me: *I don't know... but I shall try.*
Hope: *As much as love is concerned, everyone has his dosage. Don't kill yourself over it. Stay always strong, and go ahead.*

And then, she sent me by mistake, a message destined to another person, a group she was part of. We spent two to three minutes chirping about that, just to open up a little bit of our conversation.

It was strange, but Hope and I did not really have a talk on the twenty-fifth of December, Christmas day. I am sorry I couldn't sincerely remember the reason behind the respite, but nothing interesting to tell you.

Chapter 7

The New Year was quite near, and I felt as lonely as a patient infected with the worst disease ever, and that nobody, not even a fly, would like to approach. I travelled on the twenty-sixth day of the month to Ghana. In fact, I so much injected my money into obtaining the visa that I became as broke as a church mouse. Still, I managed to travel because I didn't want to see people jumping and rejoicing while I sit with my two arms buried between my legs. I have a good friend of mine called, Kaka, who was waiting for me in Ghana, also broke like me at that time.

I came to find my door opened; a door I locked before going. It was forced, not by burglars, but by my very good friend. He did so to be able to collect all the coins I left here and there inside the room. That is to tell you how critical our situation was financially. Unfortunately for him, and luckily for me, he did not even see where I saved the majority of those coins; which I brought with me, to his great disbelief. It wasn't really hidden after all. Those coins would be our savior.

Then I remembered there was something I hadn't done since I arrived. It was seventeen minutes to ten in the evening, and I wrote to Hope.

> **Me:** *I am in Ghana.*
> **Hope:** *Wow. Min bokwabor (You are welcome in fon). What about your trip? Tiresome, dear, but it is ok.*
> **Hope:** *Normal, then get some rest.*
> **Me:** *I would, but I needed to say hi to you first.*
> **Hope:** *So nice of you. I appreciate it.*
> **Me:** *You're much welcome.*
> **Hope:** *Now, get some rest.*
> **Me:** *Thank you, dear. Bye.*

Chapter 8

The following day, I was again the first person to text Hope, around thirteen minutes to 7 p.m. Someone would ask me whether I do not have other people on WhatsApp with whom I chatted. The answer is, yes, but I must confess that I chatted more with that lady than anyone else in that period. Though I cannot tell you, I was wooing her, only God knew why that attraction, until one day on the twenty-eighth of December.

> **Me:** *Good morning, firefly.*
> **Hope:** *(She sent me a smiley laughing) hummm-mmm. Good morning, President. How about the holiday?*

Me: All right, but I have a lecture this morning.
No choice.
Hope: *Sorry, dear.*
Me: Thank you, princess.

Then she repeated the key word of my message "princess" and laughed again. I didn't know what pushed me, but I suddenly bombarded her with many inquisitive questions, Why are you laughing? Are you not a princess? Am I exaggerating? Do you not deserve to be one? Hasn't anybody ever told you that you are a princess?

And she was like, "Yesssssssssssssssssss. Thank you."

I seized the chance to make some compliments. My words penetrated her, almost pierced her flexible heart, and all she was left with was, "Thank you".

I continued.

> *Me: Your profile picture is a bomb; I can't help looking at it since you placed it on your profile. You should, perhaps change it before I have a crush on you....*

She sent me a set of twenty-one laughing smileys, and promised to change it, just like that. In the next two minutes, Hope changed her profile with a nice flower. Then, I wondered why she would do something like that. We dove into some other matters and discussed them through, when I interfered into her secret life.

> *Me: Is your husband back?*
> **Hope:** *It was a lie. I don't even have a boyfriend.*

Can you imagine that lady was single, free, and not engaged? It was like I was having a dream, but she confirmed that she was not engaged. As for the ring on her finger, it was just to help stop harassments, nothing else. Before God and man, I then had the feeling that Hope could be my woman. It crossed my mind for the first time that I could date her. My heart dangled and my spirit rejoiced. I could feel it so real, and so strong. I tried to ask her some questions, which were more or less part of her private life. I suddenly felt the urge of discovering more about her. In fact, I always wanted it, but I had no solid alibi to hold on. The irony was that Hope also gave me all I needed to know about her, without any restriction. And in a jiffy, I got to know a lot more about this lady due to her sincerity and boldness. I felt like I had known her all my life, as if she had always been there for me, not too far, and not too close.

As we talked for hours that day, discussing several topics, one after another, I then realized some resemblance in our stories, of what we both went through. Weird! Knowing her deeper and deeper, I developed a pure affection and love for her. To be real, it hadn't just popped out haphazardly, but I guess that feeling had always been an inner one hidden in my heart. I couldn't dare go there, for fear of losing her completely. But then, I got a chance.

Chapter 9

On that same day, she asked.

Hope: *What is your favorite dance?*
Me: *Zouk and Slow.*
Hope: *That is for those who do not know how to dance.*
Me: *Really! And, you?*
Hope: *Agbadja (It is one of our traditional dances in Benin Rep.)*
Me: *Super. (And I laughed). God willing, you shall demonstrate it to me sometime.*
Hope: *No worry.*
Me: *What about your favorite music?*
Hope: *All types, but in a Capella.*

Me: Wow. I prefer R&B and Reggae. But as for our country music, I would say, Gota and Toba. (They are all music from Benin Rep.).
Hope: Alright. My brother rather helps me enjoy that music, but he isn't around now.
Me: Would you mind telling me your age?
Hope: May, 1987
Me: Really? I was born in that same year. Nevertheless, I am older than you.
Hope: Understood, big brother. Are you no longer going for your lecture?
Me: Sorry... it has been cancelled.
Hope: I see... So what are we going to eat?

The use of the pronoun "WE" gave me such an excitement and relief, even though I couldn't explain it, till now. Was it like, she felt the same like me, as if we knew each other for so long? It was her first time to pluralize our conversation, and I wondered what was going on in her mind. And then, I mentioned to her what my friend, Kaka, and I planned to eat that day. She complained and envied us because it is a pure local food that she confessed not having tasted since she arrived in Ghana.

That was the exact moment when the little angel suggested to me that an invitation would suite her fine, which I did by letting her choose of her free will between the thirty-first of December, and the first of January.

Hope: Like, seriously?
Me: Sure, you are invited... Are you already invited by anyone?
Hope: Alright, but I prefer the 1st of January.

Well, as you can see, I have just had my first date ever with Hope. That invitation for me was more than a mere eating and drinking occasion, or New Year chilling. I believed it could be a new starting point for me. Hope confirmed her coming and that made me the happiest man on earth. I jumped out of my bed, hailing my friend cheerfully. I briefly told Kaka everything he needed to know, till how I invited her. Fortunately, he knew her as soon as I called the name, and that actually saved me from too much explanation. I would then have to support my friend's jokes and comments about her. But all he gabbled was affirmative, because he also fancied Hope a lot based on her manners and talks at the assembly. He finally encouraged me to go out with her, as I mentioned to him it was a friendly invitation, nothing more. Thereafter, my friend and I immediately started planning what to cook in order to really please her, and making of that day an unforgettable one for her.

I came back to my phone almost an hour later, whereby some of her messages were already pending, waiting for me to answer them. I did it as quickly as I possibly could, and we carried on chatting. That was the time I also told her about my friend, Kaka, whom she seemed to know. I sent her one or two pictures of my pal to clear up her doubt. It was twelve past midday when we logged out for different reasons, in order to meet again some hours later.

At half past four, Hope and I met again online to continue what we started.

> **Hope:** *How do you often eat? Do you cook by yourself?*

Me: I normally buy food outside since I have little time for myself. Moreover, I am always exhausted before I get home in the evening. I couldn't cook under that circumstance.

Hope: Damn... so what do you plan to eat tonight?

Me: I don't know yet, perhaps rice.

Hope: And perhaps I shall come to get something and cook for you one of these days.

Me: I would fancy that.

Once more, Hope made my heart to freeze like ice. Our conversation was going so fast, as everything was falling into place. It was like a dream. Well, were it one, I never would like to wake up again. Let that dream continue forever.

Here we go again.

Hope: Get married quickly. That way, she could cook for you more often.

Me: You are not wrong. But what can I do since I have nobody for now.

Hope: Nothing, just wait.

Me: You know what?

Hope: What?

Me: From the bottom of my heart, I desire to get my woman this year and probably get her pregnant. I even told my brother, here, about it. A crazy idea, right?

Hope: Exactly what I was telling my uncle here too this morning.

Me: Really?

Hope: Yes, please. Then he asked me with whom? I replied to him – Uncle, I know I have nobody for now, but I wish to get married this year. I am tired of being alone.

Me: It is freaky.

Hope: I want to be there, at home, when my hus-
band comes back from work, let him take his
shower, give him food to eat, listen to him while
he narrates his day, advise him if need be. And
charge his "battery" (such a metaphor she used
laughing).
Me: Wow, you really mean you do not have any-
body in your life... Anyway, I like your philosophy;
a kind of woman who thinks that her husband and
children represent her world.
Hope: My universe. I wish my children took after
their father. I need to see him through them.
Me: God will give it to you. Just look around you as
you advised me earlier on.
Hope: I guess it is one way.
Me: Wow... it will be pleasant to meet someone
who is really a perfect match for our heart desire
the way you and I are doing right now, Hope. Do
you know what I think?

At that point of time, I just felt like vomiting everything; what I felt and what I wanted. I refused to
be reasonable; I mean, letting her come over before
talking about it. I couldn't even think right, think
about the consequences of what I was on the verge
of doing because I was carried away by the flame of
love, a real one.

Hope: What?
Me: It is like God is determined to punish me.
Hope: What do you mean?
Me: I like you so much... ever since I met you for
the first time. In regards to all the conversations
we've been having day after day, and particularly
today, allow me to say this: I love you. But the trav-
elling project is exactly the hindrance here. Please,

do not hate me for having told you the truth. But it is the way I feel right now. Forgive me if I messed up our relationship. I have just looked around me, as you said before, and all I see is you, Hope.

There was a long silence. Hope didn't write a word. I was perplexed and sad that I might have jeopardized what I started well till then. What would happen next? I became hopeful.

Chapter 10

January first, would Hope come as agreed?

I was no longer sure. But to my greatest surprise, Hope answered present to my invitation. It was fairly noon when my phone rang, by the time I had already finished arranging my single room, and tidied every corner to make a good impression. There was that collection of slow and romantic music I had on my computer from the first day I bought it. I thanked God I hadn't deleted it because I found its importance that very day. My phone rang and she was there, alongside the road waiting for me to take her home. Perfect timing, because food was ready and drinks too. As soon as she saw me, a large smile appeared on her face and she opened her arms for me as we got closer. There, we had our first hug, on the street, and before some people who might think we were already lovers.

I introduced her to my brother, Kaka, as we entered the house and headed to my room where Kaka would meet us twenty minutes later. The three of us behaved as normal as possible, ate and drank together as to celebrate the New Year. We had some general talks, and laughed happily. Kaka stepped out, leaving both of us to discuss what really mattered to us.

When that fastidious moment came for us to tell each other the truth, I didn't hesitate to repeat myself since I meant it. Moreover, I was determined to try all I could to win her heart. I spoke for quite a moment, while she was very attentive like a student listening to the lecturer. She looked at me regularly with the same smile she came with. On her turn, Hope took the floor by starting from her last deception and how she landed in Ghana. I felt pity for her, by the way. She gave her impression about me, and rephrased my demand. That brought to the understanding that her coming to Ghana wasn't a coincidence, but a work of God. It was planned. Before she finished, she shed some tears of joy that I removed my shirt to wipe away.

Notwithstanding, the cheerfulness within her, my proposition was still on hold. She confessed to me how scared she was; her fear of being used and dumped again, which was legitimate. I came in with arguments to convince her that I was real, and wanted something serious. She needed to feel secured and loved anew, which I was ready to offer her.

I was sitting on the mattress, while Hope was laying down with her head resting on my thighs. She tightly held on to my hand. I then looked her straight in her eyes, and said in a charming voice I tried to create.

"I do love you, Hope and wish ...."

Of course, she wouldn't let me finish. Her right hand covered my mouth.

"Please, hold me skintight in your arms," she said. "Let me feel your heartbeat."

For the second time that night, my guest of honor shed tears again.

Sometimes, maturity is not just about age, but rather through our actions and deeds. It goes without saying: "Actions speak more than words." For as long as I have been dating, Hope gave me the best "yes" answer ever. After all, we weren't children to play about the bush, but sincere on each side and grown-up enough to decide whatever was good for us. How I cherished that blessed moment because I hate begging too much for love, and hate when ladies say "no" but deep inside their heart, it is already a "yes". Hope made everything so easy and quicker for me because of the love she felt then. From then, I called her my "Sylph".

It was 9 p.m. and night had set in the sky; time for her to go back home though I wished she had spent the night with me. I understood it was our first date, and I needed to let her go because even her tutor had no idea of her whereabouts. Therefore, keeping her wouldn't be responsible at all. I called Kaka, who was unhappy, but she was going. Nevertheless he got to understanding that it wasn't proper and mannered to do so at a first date. Moreover, I wanted her forever, and not just for a single night. He and I saw Hope off to board a bus and go.

Naturally, my friend was asking me so many questions on our way home, and most importantly, whether we were by then engaged. I maintained beforehand a certain mystery about it before letting the cat out of the bag. He jumped with a delightful hurray! We both had a long talk that night as well, and Kaka wished me all the best.

It was midnight when Hope's message buzzed my cell phone:

> **Hope:** *I got home well, Mr. President, and thank you for making me happy again. Thank you, from the bottom of my heart.*

Chapter 11

The following day, our chat was much more different and casual. Yes, we then spoke to each other like a loving couple, except that my sweetheart had it difficult to address me by my name. I begged her to try because I no longer felt comfortable to hear her calling me, Mr. President. She promised to try and she did.

Does love have symptoms? I guess yes, because people out there noticed I was a changed man, happier and stronger. Many of them dared to ask me what my secret was, and I did answer to them: pure love.

On the third of January, I went to Nigeria to take my passport, whether or not I got a visa. To be honest, getting it, or not, no longer did matter to me because I had found love. God's plans are the best as long as I believe in him.

The passport in my hand, I became somewhat nervous and afraid to discover whatever the result was. I thought getting a visa would drive me far away from the woman I love. They say love at distance always has little chance to survive since we had just started; meanwhile I did not want to lose her. And in case I didn't get it, I would be wasting my money and effort, without mentioning the great opportunity I was meant to be grabbing once in Europe. As a man, I kept my fingers crossed and on a sudden move, I opened the passport without looking inside. Then, in a slow motion-like, I was about to notice it myself when my friend Ambrose said to me, "Sorry brother, take heart."

His voice echoed three times in my head while I was staring at my passport, as if it were not mine. I felt sad and bad but Ambrose was there, right beside me to console me. I gave praises to the Lord inwardly.

Then I said to Ambrose, "I am not discouraged or vanquished. I know my day will come. Let's go home, Ambrose."

Somehow, I was glad I would have the needed time to strengthen my relationship with Hope henceforth. That was my next challenge.

The same day I decided to travel to Ghana, my grandmother died at the age of one hundred. But I did not let it affect my trip though I was touched. Once in Ghana, Hope came over and we discussed our new plans and directions as a family.

Chapter 12

I started a new life with Hope in Ghana with new goals and direction. I must confess it was hectic for me at the beginning since I had planned to leave the country, but rather ended up staying. I had sold some stuffs but needed to purchase them again; I resumed all the jobs I stopped thinking about during the time I thought I would be travelling.

Hope honestly came into my life during a tough period, whereby eating, paying rent, or even satisfying her little needs as a lady was hard. I felt ashamed sometimes but she always assured me she was not a materialist. She did not come for what I had, but for what I am; that alone gave me the bravery to fight harder in order to better our situation.

Moreover, I stopped eating outside or going to bed on empty stomach. My Sylph came from time to time to cook for me, whatever the money I gave her could afford. She would struggle to get me any food I wished, even if the money I left for the cooking was not enough. In less than three months, I grew fatter. Hope regularly washed my clothes too; I would no longer need a laundrywoman.

She visited me more often and spent the night sometimes. There, I realized I should be more responsible by going to her uncles, with whom she lived. I discussed it with my better half and we made an appointment which I kept. The way her people welcomed me, and advised me that day, showed that Hope came from a kind and noble family. So, I got used to them after some time and also visited them whenever I could.

The third of May happened to be her birthday while I was not financially sound to organize anything for her. But I tried to give her a little gift in the greatest way. I bet she would never forget it, either dead or alive.

God answered our prayer for her to get a little job, which would enable her to go out. As matter of fact, she hated staying at home all day long, not to talk about her eagerness to also help financially. So for having got a job closer to my place, she decided to stay with me after talking to her uncles. I was so excited, but anxious about all we might go through once together; whether I would be able to cope with her bad manners too. Everyone has it. The truth is that I would be able to know her much more, same to her. I was afraid she might not cope with my laziness when it comes to chores, and that she would laugh at me when I heat water to take my bath every morning; she could get angry if I pick certain calls and so forth.

At the end of the day, Hope coming to live with me helped our relationship a lot. We spent some happy moments and also went through some hardship and misunderstanding; but it was all in the name of the love we felt for each other. All the moments I made her cry were not meant to hurt her, but my mere carelessness. I learned many new things about her while she also buried many of her bad attitudes. That was when we started speaking the same language and live happier.

In short, my Sylph succeeded in making me completely forget my ex.

We got engaged two years later with a bouncy baby boy, after going back to our fatherland where we came from. The child strengthened our togetherness, and we have recently got married as she always wished. It was a secret wedding; no crowd, no much expense, no unnecessary stress. It was simple but real.

We live happily together nowadays with our second child in her womb. May God help us have a daughter this time around. My wife is my life, and my family is my world.

Pure love existed, and still exists, even though it is scarce. I still think so.

Also by Franck Olivier Houngnikpo

Paperback: 80 pages
Publisher: Village Tales Publishing (April 22, 2015)
Language: English
ISBN-10: 0985362588
ISBN-13: 978-0985362584
Product Dimensions: 5.5 x 0.2 x 8.5 inches

www.ingramcontent.com/pod-product-compliance
Lightning Source LLC
Chambersburg PA
CBHW031903170626
46807CB00004B/1866